I0543047

Existentialism at the Wheel

POETRY BY ADAM GIBBS

For information contact:
Unsolicited Press
Portland, Oregon
www.unsolicitedpress.com
orders@unsolicitedpress.com
619-354-8005

Cover Design: Kathryn Gerhardt
Editor: Kristen Marckmann

ISBN: 978-1-956692-70-9

POEMS

For Lin

I stand alone by an elder tree, I do not dare breathe
Or move.
I listen.
The wheat leans back toward its own darkness,
And I lean toward mine.

—James Wright, from "Beginning"

Existentialism at the Wheel

LATE SEPTEMBER IN OHIO.

I.

Sometimes,
It does my soul a world of good
To just get away from it all,
The loneliness of the road
As opposed to the loneliness of home,
With my mind as empty
As the passenger seat next to me.

II.

I drive those long-forgotten back roads
That are everywhere in Ohio,
Roads that will be as surprised as I am
When they get to where they are going,
Unwinding through empty countryside
Littered with those old barns
That have been crumbling so long
You wonder if they were ever new.

III.

This is it,
I say to myself:
On the map of my life,
This is where everything starts to collide,
Where the setting sun starts to smolder,
And the strange orange twilight
Becomes a short, crackling fuse
On the end of a long crimson summer.

IN A DARK ROOM.

I remember the soft crackle
Of radio static in a dark room,
Quietly trying to tune the outside
World to the right frequency.

I remember the blinding light
Of a TV switching on in a dark room,
Hearing distant sirens whine towards
An emergency somewhere in the night.

I remember watching snow swirl through
Streetlights from a window in a dark room,
How it would flutter like confetti on the wind,
Celebrating how time seemed to slow.

I remember how morning light would
Change the tint of the room as it seeped in,
How the winter sunrise would make everything
Feel calm and wonderful and strange.

ADAM GIBBS

This is how I grew up in a dark room,
Where artificial light would do until
The real thing finally arrived.

CROSS STREETS.

The news says it's raining
In New York.

Cars stream through glossy streets,
Brake lights blinking ruby red
Up 42nd in Midtown,
A galaxy reflected in its own glow.

Aren't dreams high technology?
How else can you miss someplace
You've never been?

PILGRIMAGE.

There's something utterly American
About loading up the car,
Heading west through the heartland,
Searching for a distant temple
And an ancient faith, all on a modern
Highway allowing us enough space
To fill in the blanks between
Where we are
And where we want to be.

Ohio.

There's only one
Direction to go from here,
This place has
Always been a yardstick for
Westward progress, a frontier
To be mastered; from the beginning,
Before the Iroquois
Summoned their word for "great river,"

The Ohio was long since flowing west,
Searching for the sea,
Aching to be a part of the whole.

Indiana.

Crossing the state line,
Cursive hills smooth into notebook plains
As we enter country unremarkable
Yet alluring, where familiarity breeds
Both contempt and grudging admiration,
A region where everything gets flattened,
From the land to the language,
Making each vowel and every mile
Twice as long as it needs to be.

Illinois.

Plains become prairies as
We press into the Land of Lincoln,
Where Honest Abe and Stephen Douglas
Sharpened their rhetoric for battle
When words still mattered,
In the days when one

Could speak more than 280 characters
Without people feeling
Bored or insulted.

Storm clouds are forming overhead,
Outpacing us no matter how fast we drive.

Missouri.

This used to be outlaw country,
Where Jesse James and his gang
Once held sway, pioneering great
American traditions like gun violence
And upward mobility, shoe-horned
Into the very middle of the Midwest,
As if the rest of the nation simply
Had to deal with its presence,
The perfect Point B
For a journey such as this.

Rain-soaked,
The Earth apparently having
Forgiven our presumption,
We arrive at Conception Abbey,

Existentialism At The Wheel

An unlikely pilgrimage,
Proving the lengths to which
We'll go to affirm the truths that
Comprise our most human being.

ROUTE 29.

I.

It practically ran through our back yard,
Past the park at the edge of town
Where we used to shoot hoops
While cars zipped past,
Cresting the hill into the din of the city,
Or disappearing on 29
And leaving Sidney behind,
Out of sight and out of mind.

II.

One could hardly call it
"Going away" to school,
It was just one county over on 29,
But to me it seemed another country
Where everyone was fluent
In a language I couldn't speak,
So began a blue period, a year or two

Where progress ground to a halt,
Urbana seemed the last stop on 29,
And points beyond in a different orbit altogether.

III.

What once was foreign now seems familiar,
Painting with the same palette
From the earth to the sky,
Brown fields and gray clouds
Framing an open road
That unravels slowly, like an old thread:
Urbana, Mechanicsburg, West Jefferson,
I cross them off one by one,
Eastbound on 29,
Counting down the miles on my way to you.

SEA OF TRANQUILITY.

"Magnificent desolation."
—Buzz Aldrin, Apollo 11

You were a repository for our hopes,
A cosmic wishing well,
And the tokens we offered
You fell, fell, fell so far
They could not be said to have landed,
Just dissolved into a darkness so vast
Anything seemed possible within it,
Even a day when we might reach
Out and touch your face.

You showed us magnificence
In your desolation,
A peace beyond anything we'd known.
You forgave us disturbing your ancient dust,
Allowed us to wade in your tranquil sea.

And though we take you for granted still,

You continue to bounce light toward us,

Illuminating the way back,

Awaiting our return,

Eternity a moment to you.

INVISIBLE HIGHWAY.

5:30,
Hot as hell,
Dog day blues
Simmering to a boil,
The traffic is crawling
And so is your skin,
Suffering the modern
Torture of sitting still,
Eager to confront
Everyone but yourself.

So much is lost
Living in circuits,
Time becomes a plaything:
One decade you throw away,
The next gets blown to pieces.
You've got the world in your pocket,
Life in the palm of your hand,

Yet still you wander,
Driving digital roads,
Speeding down invisible highways.

Looking out from your
Room in a high-rise hotel,
Staring through your reflection,
You can hardly tell where
The lights stop and
The darkness begins.

OPEN WINDOWS.

In the night's restless quiet,
I slide through a drop-down menu
On my laptop's glowing screen
As if booking a flight,
Pointing and clicking my way around the globe.

I feel tomorrow's afternoon
Heat in New Taipei City,
Listening to the symphony of traffic
At a busy downtown intersection,
A fleet of motorbikes streaming past,
Each rider a flicker of existence,
Ghosts in the machine.

I dig my toes into the cool sand
At the Soggy Dollar,
Closed for the night
Somewhere in the British Virgin Islands,
Dead-in-the-water yachts keeping watch
Like sentinels just off the shore,

Enjoying the soothing rhythm of
Small waves washing in at my feet,
Echoes from the beginning.

I stand on an island in the controlled chaos
Of Tokyo's Shibuya Crossing,
Everyone waiting on the starter's pistol
Of the light change, then striding by in all directions,
Trying to find the shortest distance
Between here and there.

I bathe in the neon light of Times Square
As the crowd surges forward, unable to see
Where they're going above their smartphones,
Spying a young man whose thumbs
Tap furiously at the screen,
And I imagine him punching
"Live city cams" into a search engine,
Perhaps vaguely aware that,
Somewhere in the far-off suburban darkness,
Someone he'll never meet is sitting godlike,
Peering at him through open windows in the sky,
Looking down at this teeming mass
Of joy and pain below.

SKYLINE.

Driving south and west,
Racing the setting sun,
Dusk plays off dust from the fields,
A harvest of smoke and fire.

As night arrives,
The road unwinds,
Beckoning.

The Nashville skyline sparkles,
Electric clouds in a timeless sky.

LABOR DAY.

If it's the first weekend of September and you find yourself in one of the small towns folded into southeastern Ohio, you might head out just after dusk, walking down narrow, sloping streets and waving back at friendly faces chatting on wooden porches overlooking the hillsides.

If the air is thick and close, you might make your way to a downtown that feels stripped bare and untouched for decades, turning the corner beneath peeled and cracked steeples befitting a kingdom in decline, could visit the carnival that shrinks every year yet refuses to disappear.

You might trace the blinking lights down Sixth Street, weaving your way through parents calling after their children, old-timers tapping their toes to country music at the foot of the stage, and teenagers with nowhere better or worse to go.

If you come to the crest of dark oblivion at the railroad tracks, you might just turn back and take in the whole thing: the blinking, pounding, pulsing heart of a place that's been exhausted for years but keeps on going.

JEFFERSON AT MONTICELLO.

Ascending the little mountain
In the midday sun,
Bridging the centuries,
We have all of Virginia at our feet.

Like the man himself, I imagine,
The house seems almost quaint
As you approach, yet its presence
Looms once you find
Yourself within its shadow.

Precious little shade,
However, can be found nearby in
Mulberry Row, the slave quarters
Where women and men once broke
Their backs without recompense
As the man they called master
Trembled for his country.

Entering the main hall,
We step into a miniature museum
Curated by Jefferson with
Native American artifacts,
Famous paintings, and clocks of
Every shape and size adorning the walls,
Marble busts of the Founding Fathers
Studying our every step.

The first-floor walls appear to
Have been plastered with books
On every subject under the sun,
Books in French, Italian, and Latin,
Each looking as though they'd
Crumble at the slightest touch.

Wandering from room to room,
Light spills through the many windows
And fills up space within the
High ceilings and odd angles,
Contrivances of a man obsessed
With efficiency, wanting to squeeze
Every inch out of life.

ADAM GIBBS

We find ourselves in the room where
Jefferson drew his last breath,
The bed positioned at its exact center,
Ensuring everything remained within his orbit.

Making our way past an
Improbably narrow staircase, my pulse quickens
As I have a vision of the old sage himself,
Weary with age, climbing the stairs in the night.
A lone candle lighting his way,
His bones aching with each step,
Yet his mind still racing
Like Monticello's many clocks,
Turning and moving with precision,
Ticking toward a future at once
Unknown and unknowable,
Ineffable,
Inevitable in the course of human events.

NIGHT DRIVE.

At this hour,
Northwest Missouri may as well be
The far side of the moon,
Foreign, uncharted,
No stars or satellites to steer by,
No cities soaked in the sepia of their streetlights,
No faint red beacons pulsing
From atop radio towers,
Not even a single house emitting
The warm glow of familiarity.

Darkness,
The great equalizer,
Has leveled the landscape,
We're moving forward
But the enveloping night obscures our progress
Beyond the car's electric eyes.

"Where are we?"

With affectation stripped away,

The question resonates

But the answer remains elusive,

Taillights fading in the rear-view

As we press on,

Farther and further into the void,

Filling in the blank spaces,

Writing our lyrics to the rhythmic hum

Of life's relentless machine.

UP WITH THE STATIC.

If context shapes a life,
Language is our last best hope,
A technology which can never be unlearned.

The language is shrinking,
Compressed in the vice-grip of instant gratification,
Relegated from the airwaves,
Reduced to fit in the space between the stations where,
If you turn the dial slowly,
The static seethes and pops like primitive music.

The language is raging,
Pouring in buckets like a summer storm,
Saturating everything but
Evaporating almost as quickly in
The simmer of postmodern drought.

The language is ascendant,
A rocket so powerful it has escape velocity,
Capable of hurtling us free from our gridlock
Into the stratosphere of pure possibility.

WINTER MORNINGS.

Standing at the window in a sleepy house,
Looking out into the late December night
On the checkerboard of frosted rooftops,
Chimneys hissing steam,
The spiderweb of dead trees
Looming gracefully in the distance,
I peer through that cold and holy darkness
Back to those days when
We understood little of sacrifice,
Even less how precarious life was,
Past and present held together
By the logic of a dream.

I remember he used to ferry us through town
On winter mornings, safely transporting
Us from one warm house to another.
We couldn't feel the strain in his arms
When he stooped to pick us up,
The weight of the world he kept to himself,
Bones aching with integrity.

Nodding off in the back seat,
We had no way of knowing
The hands on the wheel could work miracles,
Teaching us love's language
Before we even understood the words.

THIS CRUEL WAR.

History, despite its wrenching pain,
Cannot be unlived, and if faced
With courage, need not be lived again.
—Maya Angelou, "On the Pulse of Morning"

As the bay glitters magnificent
In midday December,
We leave the harbor behind,
The clop of carriage horses fading from earshot,
Bound for the tiny speck of Fort Sumter on the horizon.

Once upon the island, I hold my wife's hand
Walking amid eroded brick and dormant cannons,
A scene so tranquil you could almost believe
This cruel war was as romantic as you've been told.

Later that afternoon,
Filing through the tomblike quiet
Of the Old Slave Mart Museum,
I linger over a glass case containing

A rusted pair of chain-linked shackles,
Instruments of torture
That once cut into human flesh
And weighed down many thousands gone.

All around us,
Our solemn parade continues its circle,
Surrounded by history.

THE DARK HUNG HEAVY ABOVE ME.

After Ginsberg

The dark hung heavy above me
In an apartment on the edge of town,
At an hour when night and morning
Had called a brief truce,
And I was thinking I'd rather be
Anywhere but here,
Rather be driving the back roads of Illinois
At dusk with nowhere to be,
Rather sing hallelujah on the banks
Of the Mississippi in Memphis,
Rather fall from grace in St. Louis,
Rather lose my nerve
At a sidewalk café in Iowa City,
Rather feel anointed under the bar lights
In Minneapolis and stumble drunk
Back to my hotel room alone,
Rather wake up forgetting
Who I was in Sioux Falls,

Rather feel the cold snow
Stinging my cheeks in downtown Topeka,
Rather pace like a caged animal
Amid the slots of a Tulsa casino,
Rather get lost driving through the prairie
West of Amarillo and have the guy
Behind the gas station counter laugh
When I ask for directions,
Rather have expensive cocktails
At a rooftop party in Santa Fe while
Listening to artists argue about sincerity,
Rather ascend body and soul in Boulder,
Rather lock my key in my room in Salt Lake City,
Rather have a glimpse of perfection in Cheyenne,
Rather feel the warm breeze with the windows
Down as I speed past Reno's neon bulbs,
Rather see the morning fog burning off
Above the trees in wine country near Sonoma,
Rather taste the salt as I dive head-first
Into the Pacific at Big Sur,
Rather turn the car around in San Francisco
And point it east toward the future,
Rather drive and drive and drive,
Rather withstand wave after wave
Of American dreams as I head back,

Almost home but not yet,

Still plenty of time to wonder what's next,

Still plenty of time to imagine
Who I'll be until the day I die.

THE ROAD TO SLEEP.

I.

My insomnia used to take me strange places.
Always the last one awake after a party,
I'd wander dark rooms
And hallways of my host's dwelling,
An anthropologist observing
Some ancient civilization,
Silently moving through the house
As the TV glowed with some infomercial
Or a movie I had seen a thousand times.
Each food container sitting out in the kitchen,
I'd scrutinize.
Every portrait hanging in the living room,
I'd consider at length.
Stacks of magazines on coffee tables,
I'd thumb through.
I was studying something I was part of
Yet felt so distant from,
Wandering the wrong way on the road to sleep.

II.

Working nights
Made the days seem sinister,
Midsummer light pressing in,
Creeping around my blackout curtains
As I waited for the pills to kick,
For that wave to wash over me,
Carrying me away to sleep's distant shore.

III.

I was on my way the first time
You fell asleep in my arms,
My breathing slowing to sync with yours.
I was halfway there when I'd wake
Just long enough in the changing light
To feel your warm body next to mine.
And now I return each night
To meet you in blessed darkness,
Sleeping the sleep of the saved and thankful.

PERSPECTIVE.

There's no squaring that circle
That begins as a child when you
Wonder how something as small
As your thumb eclipses the entire sun,
Which better minds have already
Assured you is so very big.

The lens through which you view
The world is in constant flux,
Its magnification changing
Since time immemorial,
Leaving certain mysteries
Just out of reach,
Lost in the middle distance,
Lingering like shadows at dusk.

Your memories are made and remade,
Rearranged every time a new truth
Conquers an old one,
The feeling of walking

EXISTENTIALISM AT THE WHEEL

Outside the morning after a storm,

When the world looks the same

But feels just a little different,

The air having been swept clean

For the next breath you gladly take in.

COMING DOWN IN BOSTON.

I.

I was present at the creation,
Here since the beginning.
Long before Boston ever burst to life
In a fluorescent blur outside this airborne window,
I was there slumbering in the sea just beyond,
Buried down in the depths we came from.
But I've always felt more at home like this:
Head lost in the clouds,
Building castles from the sky down.

II.

Ohio,
To paraphrase one poet,
Always seems to lie just north of the way things are.
What are you to do when flyover country is home?
Your hands become a map of the world,

Each line a river viewed from thirty thousand feet,
Earth's bloodlines forever flowing back into her ocean heart.

III.

Touching down in Boston,
Feet finally on the ground.
Flight 1080 arriving on time,
I've come back around.

WAITING ON THE SURGEON.

How can a place that saves lives feel so lifeless?

The quiet chorus of footfalls on cold tile. Harsh lights and dull shades. The sterile scent of rubbing alcohol on stainless steel.

Isn't there a song about the smell of hospitals in winter?

Glancing at the vague, non-threatening artwork on the wall, I wonder if ever there was an artist who dreamed of painting something that made people feel nothing at all.

The surgeon glides into the waiting area like an apparition in his white lab coat, drawing little gasps all around. He tells us the procedure went well, then describes it with a calm detachment I find unsettling. I never thought I'd hear someone matter-of-factly begin a sentence with, "When the heart is empty…" After that, his words just sort of dissolve into static.

"He's lucky, isn't he?" a relative asks.

The surgeon gives a meandering non-answer, a noble evasion from a man who must've begun far too many conversations with the words "I'm so sorry" to believe in anything as quaint as luck.

We sit in silence after he disappears. It's one of those maddening silences that reminds you the universe is always listening but owes you no explanations, and that if luck even exists it is only in that we are outrageously lucky to have ever been born at all.

SOMEWHERE, IT'S MORNING.

Somewhere, it's morning,
Constellations are fading
And the day breaks pregnant with hope,
With all the terrible beauties of possibility.

Somewhere, it's morning,
Constellations are fading
And people are left with no choice
But to confront one another in the light,
Mapping out the foreign policy of their lives
Full of intrigue and betrayal,
Red-handed proof the human heart is in constant rebellion,
Always beating against its borders.

Somewhere, it's morning,
Constellations are fading
And people are trying their hands at diplomacy,
Refusing to believe the persistent fiction
That more can be solved by not talking to each other
Than by talking to each other.

Somewhere, it's morning,
Constellations are fading
But Cassius is still right:
The fault is not in our stars,
But in ourselves.

So sleep now,
And let the darkness do its sacred work.

WALKING THROUGH THE CITY AT NIGHT.

You have to stand close to see the
Brushstrokes of a city, to feel the texture of
Each moment, to discover what the darkness holds.

Rainfall on concrete, glistening glass,
People making their way to what's next.

Shoulder to shoulder, sleeve to sleeve,
Collecting mementos from strangers like a pickpocket:
The flash of a smile, a burst of laughter,
Overlapping stories that never end or begin,
Voices that fade like disappearing ink,
Words written on air.

DISPATCHES FROM THE END OF HISTORY.

1991

Someone had changed the channel, this wasn't our usual Sunday night viewing. I remember the faint outline of buildings washed in night vision green, an ominous tint my generation would grow used to. Suddenly, the screen went violently, blindingly white, as if a bulb had burst within the TV. The adults in the room inhaled sharply but no one spoke. Even at six years old, I knew something had changed. "This war is gonna be easy," someone finally said.

2001

There's something different about the drone of plane engines overhead now, some imperceptible menace, terrible echoes that never fully recede. That creeping fear when a stranger looms over your shoulder in a crowd, that vague dread that rises when the engines fire for takeoff. You can't put your finger on it, but it's there, something you can't quite trust about an impossibly blue September sky.

2020

A day is coming when cable news won't break in for mass shootings because they've become regularly scheduled programming. A day is coming when you can experience a terrorist attack through your VR goggles, when you can cast your ballot via text while shopping for Christmas presents on Amazon. A day is coming when islands disappear under water, when this sinking planet will leave us no choice but to take the high ground in an argument nobody can win.

MY NEIGHBORS SINGING.

I'm always forgetting the mail in summertime,
Venturing out into muggy twilight
When the sky is pale blue and burning at the edges.

Tonight, the mailbox's bang-and-clatter
Is accompanied by a sweeter sound,
Voices rising melodically from a nearby window.

Looking down at postmarks from far away,
I pause to listen as they reach up to catch the breeze,
Touching every bit of the evening air,
A blessing.

WEATHER APP.

There must be a bug in the software,
I can smell the gears smoking from here.
This technology doesn't know its own strength.

I'm getting weather reports from the North Pacific,
Adrift in that deep blue immensity,
An island equidistant from everywhere.

How's the weather where you are?
72 and sunny, clear as a bell.

I should be floating into range soon,
A blip at the edge of some distant screen,
Faintly pulsing.

BRAIN FOG.

I've been losing the plot
                        all summer long, flipping
in a panic to check the   facing page,
clicking refresh
on thoughts
                        shaped like doorways
                to   empty rooms.

Are you there?

I've seen you creeping
                        like a premonition at the edge
of my vision, felt your sleeve brush
                                my
                                        arm
like a stranger in the crowd,
heard you in the din and
        roar
of life's relentless machine.

Can you hear me?

I caught a glimpse of you just now
on the highway circling
the   city,
            watching the sunset in
                            high glass,
strange orange twilight filtering
through the canyons.

Is this our exit?
Hands at 10 and 2.
Try to keep it between the lines.

FALLING ASLEEP WITH THE TV ON.

Last I remember, the weatherman was calling for rain, a seventy percent chance, emerald green pixels drifting over half of Ohio. Maps and mathematics can't hold me now, my mind an untethered balloon, I feel like I'm floating slowly out in space, a lonely satellite pinging signals back to Earth. The sports desk says the game is in overtime, that the home team is up against it, that sometimes a draw can feel like a win. I think there's breaking news coming in, it's so hard to tell these days. Gunshots accompanied the last song of the night, an airplane has disappeared without a trace. The seas are still rising, a bomb has gone off somewhere far away. Content loading, please wait, skip this ad in five seconds, the video already has a million views. We still say things have gone viral, even during a plague. The death toll is rising but we remain unfazed, large numbers don't scare us anymore. The hush of static dulls my senses, but I can still hear the flicker of voices peeling through. They say the returns are coming in, one percent reporting, please stand by, we have a big projection to make.

When I wake, the rain has turned to snow. The noon sky looks like a deep well, the frozen earth mirrored glass. A commentator says the parade is about to start. Is that cheering I hear in the distance? The weatherman says it's turning colder, that this winter may run long.

LITTLE THINGS.

After Maggie Smith

What kind of monster are you if
You've never waved someone on
At a four-way stop?

How many lives have you lived if
You've never pulled a library book off the
Shelf and thumbed through it
Without really knowing why?

Are we speaking the same language?
You understand, don't you?

If this poem is a stone covered
With ancient glyphs, walk away.

If you've never stepped out into
A blinding summer sun and told

Your friend how bright it is,
I want little to do with you.

You've thrown your arms around
Someone and told them it's OK when
You had no idea if it was OK, haven't you?

You feel those echoes far down,
In depths only you have access to.

You're right to feel vulnerable;
Forget them, I'm with you.

After all,
If the spirit doesn't enter the room
Along with your favorite song,
What's the point?

ACKNOWLEDGMENTS

"Open Windows" and "The Dark Hung Heavy Above Me" first appeared in The Mark Literary Review (Edition Ten, September 2019)

"Perspective" first appeared in Dumb Luck (Gibbs, Unsolicited Press, 2020)

"Late September in Ohio" first appeared in Voyage of the Mind (September 2020)

"Dispatches From the End of History" first appeared in The Mark Literary Review (Edition 24, November 2020)

"Falling Asleep With the TV On" first appeared in Second Chance Lit (Issue 1, January 2021)

So much has happened since the world went into lockdown in those dizzying days of March 2020. I used the extra time at home to put together this manuscript and send it out into the world. Just as they did with *Dumb Luck*, Unsolicited Press believed in this project and I'm eternally grateful to them for all they've done to help get these poems to you.

In a time of constant change and uncertainty, I've been blessed to have my beautiful family keep things in perspective for me. My daughter Clara puts her arms around me and says she loves dada. My son Isaac never stops smiling. And my wife Lindsay is our North Star, the light our family steers by. Nobody has ever believed in me as fiercely as she has. This book is for her.

BIBLIOGRAPHY

On the Pulse of Morning, Maya Angelou (Random House, 1993)

Collected Poems 1947—1997, Allen Ginsberg (HarperCollins, 2010)

Above the River: The Complete Poems, James Wright (Farrar, Straus and Grioux, 1992)

Poem Beginning with a Retweet, Maggie Smith (Colorado Review, Volume 46, Number 2, Summer 2019)

ABOUT THE AUTHOR

Adam Gibbs is an author and poet from Grove City, Ohio. His writing has appeared in The Mark Literary Review and Second Chance Lit. His novella, Dumb Luck, is available from Unsolicited Press. He lives with his wife Lindsay and their two children, Clara and Isaac.

ABOUT THE PRESS

Unsolicited Press is based out of Portland, Oregon and focuses on the works of the unsung and underrepresented. As a womxn-owned, all-volunteer small publisher that doesn't worry about profits as much as championing exceptional literature, we have the privilege of partnering with authors skirting the fringes of the lit world. We've worked with emerging and award-winning authors such as Shann Ray, Amy Shimshon-Santo, Brook Bhagat, Kris Amos, and John W. Bateman.

Learn more at unsolicitedpress.com. Find us on twitter and instagram.